WRITING FLORA,

WRITING FAUNA

A Collection of Poems by Poets
of the Southern San Joaquin Valley

in collaboration with

The Walter Stiern Library

at

California State University, Bakersfield

2018

Many thanks to Curt Asher at the Walter Stiern Library
for his ongoing enthusiasm and support of poetry.

Previous issues of the "Writing" series
can be found in the Walter Stiern Library collection
at California State University, Bakersfield.

Writing Work (2017)
Writing the Drought (2016)

Edited by Matthew Woodman

Cover Illustration, "Rufous hummingbird,"
by Karissa Garcia

WELCOME

Chemically speaking, you are virtually indistinguishable from an oak. Or from an octopus, for that matter. Hydrogen, oxygen, carbon, and nitrogen (with a tiny percentage of other elements thrown in for luck) comprise all we know of life. Even our DNA, what we swab and send through the mail to trace our genealogies, illustrates that we are a 60% match to . . . the banana.

The old cliché "you are what you eat" is true . . .

We here in Kern County live in one of the nation's biodiversity hotspots, encompassing a significant number of diverse geological features, from the California Coast Range to the Tehachapi Mountains to Death Valley to the Sierra Nevada, featuring chaparral, oak woodland, Joshua Tree woodland, shadscale scrub, alkali sink, valley grassland, and forest ecosystems. As for our endangered endemics, most of us are familiar with the San Joaquin Kit Fox, but have you considered the burrowing owl, the Barstow woolly sunflower, the Tehachapi slender salamander?

One protein all organisms share is Cytochrome C, an essential component of respiration. Think of this shared fellowship, this communal gear whirring deep within your cells, as you read these poems, as these words aspire to breath and the celestial firing of synapse deep within the dual hemispheres you carry with you wherever you go.

CONTENTS

The People's Fauna

The Dust began it;
the Dust will end it:
The winding road goes on
Tracks litter the Trodden path
Retraced countless times
How many imprints linger here
Among the almond trees
Within the citrus groves?
Little Boxes line the trails
Beings dwell within
Some frames are TALL and others *slim*
Or **w i d e** or short or ~trimmed~
With great décor! or poor.
The shining stars are dazzling yet dim
Hordes of gold uncovered
Yet no treasure lies within
The empty caves; still,
Where two or three are gathered
More will surely come
To join the throngs and folds
Stones all sized the same
Lie here all gathered 'r**O**und
one final **R**equiem
Inklings **P**resent from time now gone
for the Dust began it;
the Dust will end it:
To *Ash* all must return…

--Sera Bethany

Tumble Dry Low

rock'n'rollin' down the street
  not caring what others have to say
   - doing my own thing my own way -
     under scorching sun when all the land is parched
I will tumble dry low to say 'hello'

always causing trouble
  the #rough-and-tumble-guy
   I travel with the wind ~
    I travel with the breeze ~
     so fear those heat-filled days
      fear my tangled weave 'cause
I will tumble dry low to say 'hello'

when summer heats the air: I see them
  in their eyes fear and *hatred* gleam
   they see me yet see me not
    I am a *blight* to them
     by my nature in itself
      so they avoid me like the plague
    but still!
I will tumble dry low to say 'hello'

low to the ground still tall enough
  to rip to $S_HR^ED_S$ all in my path
   I laugh out loud grating metal with my teeth
    then I am gone with the summer breeze ~
     for as I roll so am I **dead**
      yet when you want to say
    "goodbye"
I will tumble dry low to say 'hello'

--Sera Bethany

For Lauretta

lupines used to grow
through the rocks on the hill
next to Mimi's house
and she would always comment on their beauty
and when the wind blew
the lupines would dance
to Patsy Cline
crazy
and then the poppies flared
their soft silk petal gold cups
open to the sky
waiting to be filled with blue milk
together the flowers formed a quilt
across the red clay
burned in my memory
until we meet again
I will continue to water the seeds
in the soil
you enriched
they will grow more beautiful than the ones
you remember
and the quilt will sing in yellow and blue
long after I'm gone
for my daughter and my son

--Sherean Bledsoe

My Daughter Chose

the shiny deep turquoise blue
Dragon Scaled Betta fish
because he spoke to her somehow

a mirror reflecting back to my foundation

I live for you

a smaller better version
of myself

that fish built a bubble nest
we learned together
that's what the male Betta Fish do

when they are happy

--Sherean Bledsoe

Yellow

My beautiful Blazing Star,
Erupting from the stones like a
Newborn, bouncing with life,
Trembling for the chance to reach
Zenith. The heavens where you belong.
Epitome of survival, stamens
Longing for connection, stretching
Indiscriminately toward
Another.

Last love of
Adam, creation so divine
Even in the confines of the desert, proven
Veritably inhospitable, you
Invoke life: Grow. Go.
Catch the breeze to
Another plot of sand,
Utilizing yet another unlivable locale.
Latching onto the lips of the sun,
Inciting photosynthesis,
Salvaging morsels to make a meal.

--Greg Bolanos

Admiration

Oviparous fish grow up
Without a father.
Their mothers abandon them
Before they've been born.

Zooplankton is scarce,
Many starve in the larval stage.

From fry to fingerling,
Juveniles are valuable
Only
When fully matured.

They look up to those caught,
Because at least they are desired
As: Food. Pets. Dried out Decor.

But we all know Finding Nemo
Is a fantasy.
Fish don't have friends.
They hardly have parents,
Dory certainly didn't have any.
Some drop out of schools
To join shoals.
Pain is more real than love,
Ask Temple Grandin.
And life is in color.

But don't be fooled,
As the fish are,
The Golden Trout is a
Gilded Bronze.

--Greg Bolanos

Maintaining a Place in the Evaporating Water Table:
On Drinking During the Firestorms

Much wooded suburban creek-land, char, ashes
and stonework—mule deer are more naked
for their ability to outrun fire on a cautious
diet of leaves, berries and horticultural acreage.

"Flames cannot extinguish our joy," I tell my Zin.
Yet with us only a reflection of the depths
of the Milky Way remains—a lit sky atrium
in one half-finished glass. Like streetlights the trees are dead.

So many do not yet even know if they know two facets
about the people disappearing each morning with fled swans
from redwood canals or kit foxes off burnt valley pastures.

Yet Angelinos, Mendocinites, Napans and Sonomans, all
after rain cools each neighborhood with its late response
again sow their every mineral to this new layer with resolve.

--Jeremy Casabella

Redleg Frog

Shaking a hiccup
into distant listeners
with a puckered cling peach

of unripe face,
sepia at rest in its
bruised skin as

inebriate as gold,
each gulps at moonlit buoyancy

to uncouple
the colossal dream.

--Jeremy Casabella

Sycamore

In the night,
Arm-like branches reach up to the stars and
to the brightest light, the almost full moon,
and tenderly grasp the sacred openness of eternity.

With the cold, the green leaves turn brown, sapped of warm fluid.
The leaves dry and die into brittle brownness.

The sycamore leaves flutter, then drift like snowflakes,
hundreds in a flurry—each one unique.

With winter's rain, more and more leaves drift down.
Wind sweeps the fallen leaves against the back porch glass door.
Hundreds of leaves nudge each other and peep into the family room.

      I opened the door, and brought a leaf in,
      a brown large hand-like partial-star with five points;
      Its palm-side is smooth and glistens in reddish hue;
      The other side is furry softness.
      I tap the dry leaf repeatedly, a duet of connection-thou and I.
      I go into the yard and look - up at the barren branches.
      I feel the warmth of the sun and the drifting breeze.

With warmth from the sun in the new season,
clusters of nascent leaves burst on the stems.

--Portia Choi

Geococcyx californianus

Such wonder, the greater roadrunner, with its zygodactyl foot, four toes with two facing forward and two facing back. It confuses a predator who wonders, "where did that crazy bird go? Did it go this or that way?"

True to its family name, cuculidae, the roadrunner drives the Wylie Coyote a bit cuckoo. At least in the cartoons.

I saw a real roadrunner, for the first time, in the yard of Ridgecrest's Maturango Museum.

I was walking a labyrinth, a one-way path of curves and straight lines leading from the outer circle to a center; a path outlined by local rocks. I took each step slowly - - slowly, in meditation.

I wondered what it would feel like to walk over the rocks. (No one would see whether I stayed on the path or not.) But I obeyed the unenforceable and stayed between the rocks, taking one step, then another, then more steps to the center. Then I retraced the steps back to the outer edge of the labyrinth.

I then sat on a bench, breathing slowly, looking at the rocks of the labyrinth from a distance. They looked gathered together, without any path in between them.

Then I saw a bird scurrying across the rocks. Its tail seemed to wave at me. It followed its own path, straight across the rocks, from one edge of the labyrinth to the other.

Oh such fun, "Beep-beep, cuckoo, beep-beep, cuckoo, cuckoo, cuckoo, cuckoo."

--Portia Choi

Lotus Rising

Fibrous roots embedded deeply in wet Earth
A firm anchor
Purpose

Hollow buoyant stems surrounded by rippling Water
A life sustainer
Abundance

Leaves and buds reaching for pure Air
A primal longing
Desire

Petals unfurling into a ring of Fire
A burning up
Liberation

Infinite Immortal Bliss manifesting in Eternal Void
A conscious Universe
Absolute

-- Priti Devaprakash

Fight or Flight

The wings of my heart beating frantically
More than eighty times per second

The restless hum of which renders me deaf

To the outside world

Moving in a figure-eight pattern
The symbol of infinity

Fear without end
Every moment an eternity

Hovering stationary in physical space
Thoughts flitting in constant motion

Desperately seeking nectar to dull the pain
As if life depends upon it

Fighting to fly

Flying not to fall

-- Priti Devaprakash

Golden Trout (*Oncorhynchus mykiss aguabonita*)

Riding low
   up the mouth
of the Killer
on past the coccyx-
splintering Zeppelin,
we swerve
   above the brackish
   green river
stopping when
spotting, just short
of fallin'
off nearly
sheer granite
   from brink to bank
where beneath
   waters are California's
trout,
golden
and storied.

Amid the young,
I sank
on a crevice,
   commandeered
a line, and
watched
the waters
reflecting
   the sky
in depths
   I
could
   not
fathom.

Faking frivolity
opened
adventure;
   I became
the pioneer
and master

of nature,
　　in handcuffs,
that day.
the trout was
a compassionate
trout.
　　Catch
and release.

--Jeff Eagan

She Is Hyperion!

Still budding, still weak
Still fragile, still bleak
Still a misconstrued physique
Polluted by practiced technique
Still this has been on repeat

Still the growth is stunted
Still the strength is hunted
And, still, it's discarded in the mud
Undug by anyone
Still nothing but a rerun

Desire and its pursuit
To grow past just the roots,
Both manners to execute

Murders that have been made absolute.
Will the blooming ever see anything but the bottom of a workman's boot?
Will they ever step off and let her see herself anew?

They saw her a dandelion, a weed
A bud that, although pretty,
And perhaps a decently scented,
Only whenever the time to smell was presented,
Would only serve for the eyes to see

Nothing more than, nothing less than
A pleasure to look at
You're better off with just grass

But, no, not this one.

The one who grew past
Showed that they looked and stepped far too fast
For, from the womb of Gaia,
She is Hyperion!
Their unworthy flower
A new tower to feast their eyes on

With the stench of a skunk instead of the scent of a rose
To drive off the pests that want her to erode

Mineral wool, the clothing resting on her skin
Against her, raging flames will never win
Historically torn roots founded a body so sturdy
An axe couldn't make the smallest dent
A bulldozer would find itself bent

The more she holds strong
Against pressed vulnerability that's been lifelong
The more and more Hyperion evolves long
To see past the garden that thought of her wrong

Unfortunately her height is almost forbidden to be seen,
Something so coarsely beautiful
Could make eyes bleed
And demolish the workman's reality

But fortunately for she, blood never dripped to make her blind
Growth opened her eyes
To everything
She realized her preceding invisibility,
The ways workmen sunk her in the ground quietly

But still, she stands calm
And still, she stands strong
Amongst chaos, and war, and destruction, and all
A branch reaches out to those who sought her downfall

Because a murder is a murder
Even if they tried to deroot you first
Infecting a wound
Will only make it worse

So she offers her tokens,
Water, sheath, and air
To reforest
The peace that should be there

But if they dare
Begin to step, begin to tear, begin to impair
And, again, claim her as theirs,
She now has the strength
She now has the height,
Not to fight, but to look above

And settle elsewhere.

No longer sweet, no longer small,
No longer feeble, no longer young
Permanently tall, the highest of them all,
She grew to be Hyperion!

--Zeltzin Estrada-Rodriguez

The Dogs Howl

You can hear the cries from time to time
Disturbing serene sleep under the moon
Disrupting peaceful stillness on a sunlit cloudless day
Keep them outside because inside they might not do their business right
That's what you think they're like

Fortunate are the ones that are kept inside when it's black
The others make ice wind their best friend
Fortunate are the ones that are kept inside when it's burning
The others feel their hair ignite

The first of the others to break the silence
Gains the response of ripples
An echo of their insides
Shared desire to be inside

They've seen few escape past the bars and make it back alive
Someone blind to the common chase
Towards a stride that's self-sustained
Leave many dead before they've experienced the other side

Glory be
That they have each other to hear their screams
Glory not
When they reap their brother's heavier fur to keep them warm
Glory not
When they tear their sister's skin off and use it for shade
Glory not
When a common kin is picked apart

--Zeltzin Estrada-Rodriguez

The California Least Tern

The Browni, *Sternula Antillarum*,
Breeds in bays of the Pacific Ocean.
Related to the little tern of the Old World,
It wears a black cap; its bill points downward.

It has a white belly, pale gray wings and back;
Flies with fast, jerky wingbeats and a hunchback.
At 8 to 9 inches and 1.5 ounces small,
Its syrinx produces an odd, squeaky call.

It can fly at 4 weeks with a 20-inch wingspan,
But this bird is vulnerable to disturbance by man
And natural disasters. Put on the endangered list,
Its numbers have increased with protected status.

Nests can often be seen along the marine shore;
The clutch is usually 2 or 3, sometimes 4.
Both parents incubate the eggs for 3 weeks
And together tend the semi-precocial chicks.

The tern family is adapted to sandy beach nesting
Lined with tiny sticks, shells, and seaweed, for resting.
Well camouflaged in its natural habitat,
To ward off predators, it will mob or harass.

The tern hunts in lagoons and shallow estuaries
For smelt, silversides, surfperch, and anchovies.
It will hover until spotting its prey and then dive
Into the sea to extract the fish, eat, and survive.

--Shelley Evans

Rose-Flowered Larkspur

Delphinium Purpusii is the scientific name
Of the plant called Rose-Flowered Larkspur.
It's a rare species endemic to Kern County
Where the Sierra Nevada meets the Mojave Desert.

Growing wild on the rocky cliffs and in the talus,
Unusually bright pink among this mainly blue genus;
A perennial herb, also known as a dicot,
Its stem is thin with a cluster of flowers on top.

It matures to reach a height of ½ to 1 meter,
And there are 10 to 20 blossoms on each one.
Its sepals curl either forward or backward
As its round leaf blades soak up the sun.

Each flower has 5 petal-like sepals
That grow together, forming a spur-
Ended pocket, which gives this plant its name,
A dolphin-shaped place to store nectar.

From late spring to late summer it blooms,
Pollinated by hummingbirds and bumble bees.
Although toxic to humans and livestock,
It's used as food by larvae of some species.

Also named the Kern County Larkspur,
This plant is in the buttercup family
That survives in a narrow zone of landscape
Within the Red Rock Canyon State Park boundary.

--Shelley Evans

Rose

She sits there, peacefully.
Occasionally swaying back and forth
As the forceful winds
Of winter nights approach.

She sits there, puzzled.
Not knowing her purpose,
Nor understanding the means
Of her existence.

She sits there, impatiently
Waiting upon his arrival.
Hoping he'll finally act
On his temptation.

Dressed in red,
So radiant.
So exquisite.
Blemishes nonexistent.

Bursting of exotic beauty,
She screams, settling the voices
Of those around her.
She is the outspoken one
Sitting quietly among the ones
Less talked about.

Although grown, she blooms
At the sight of him.
Observation is no longer enough.
He must have her. Cherish her.
Not just momentarily, rather,
For all of eternity.

He reaches for her- nature's gift,
Finally ceasing to resist the urge.
Carrying her away,
She sits peacefully in palm.
No longer impatient.
No longer puzzled.

--Andrea Franco

Remembrance

Mid-summer July
Careless lovers, hand-in-hand
fall for Honolulu's beauty;
Waist-deep, warm waters
Too much a dream
for the Mainland.

Fast-forward five hours,
Croon along to Jack Johnson
On Kamehameha highway—
"Wait! Slow down and admire the
Birds of Paradise: most beautiful flower,"
from the lips of the
most beautiful boy.

Fast-forward five years
California Coastin'
The smallest glimpse, a faint head-turn
An orange hue and contrasting blue
from the Crane's mouth—
Alone.
And yet, a smile broadens,
Rolled-down windows allow the breeze pass through,
Eyes shut, Bob Marley serenades
Three little birds.

--Karissa Garcia

All Mortals Are Grass

A voice proclaims:
All mortals are grass.
A dispiriting metaphor
Sure to foment
Dissent or green-eyed envy
Of the wild flower
Preening in a field.

But about that proud flower
Swaying to windy rhythms,
A voice again proclaims:
Death will surely blast
Both grass and flower.
The ordinary will wither,
The beautiful fade.

--Jack Hernandez

Sluggards and Ants

Go to the ant, you sluggard,
see its ways and get wisdom.
(Proverbs 6:6)

There's a lesson here:
The ant gets the house,
car, girl, and praise
from other ants, bees, worms
who march, fly straight, and dig
through the passing of daily time.
The sluggard pitied, occasionally
reviled as morally slack,
gets only the odd, surprising
detour, the scent of flowers
lounged upon, and the feel
of lazing in wet, cool earth.

--Jack Hernandez

Into the Dearth

Before the waters vanished
this glebe
breathed with sweet green grasses,
and bragged with purple clover,
spikelets of foxtail
and orange poppies.

This morning,
whilst traipsing the dusty foothills just outside of town,
I acknowledge the afflictions of a five-year drought.
Sand spouts terrorize the scant vegetation in the distance
and black balls of spiky tumble weed
feign good cheer,
all the while,
anticipating the inevitable shattering
raked away by bulldozers
smashed into thorny bits
the final degradation of what might have been

Sluggish, the land lies prostrate
with feeble prayer,
a brittled yellowing grass
afraid to ask for too much,
hoping for just enough.
A repartee of vague breezes ridicule their yoked existence,
granting only a dust of disappointment
to settle in the furrow of unheard supplication
and unending heat.

Almost inconceivably,
a thirsty thunder explodes against
the clutter of a confused sky.
Dappled clouds trundle,
whirling with the grumble
of an empty storm.
The fretful savannas
yearn for the prodigal tears
to inspirit a forsaken salvation,
with the promise of an unfolding rain.

Hoping against hope.

Hope, afterall,
is the language of all living things
tethered to a desperate past.

--Anke Hodenpijl

Guttersnipe

pushed to the outside margins
they shelter
hunched in the shadows
behind dumpsters and garbage cans
waiting for the inevitable do-gooder
to offer a Big Mac or leftover fries

finding refuge in the dry brush along the freeways
in makeshift colonies
they survive unnoticed by those
with purpose, place and mission
catching fleeting glimpses of another life
yet paying attention to none of it
only folding into
what is left of the wild

the San Joaquin kit fox
with lanky body, colossal ears
and gangling legs
dodge spears of light along the interstate
and recoil from the hissing sounds of traffic

If I don't kill them?
If I feed them kibble?
If I toss out leftovers?
If I say they are endangered?
If I notice how cute they really are?
If I admit my progress meant their demise?

Would that be enough atonement?
Or do they need a sign like the homeless,

Hungry

Alone.

--Anke Hodenpijl

I Think Every Squirrel

He runs around
And they always try to hunt him down
His voice annoying
I think he really loves the sound
His passion climbing
He's always on some ups and downs
He buries feelings
I swear he stuffs them underground

--Chad Johnson

Wings

Even the ugly start out simple
With six legs and no spine
Looking for the sun
They seek to shine

Can't see they're special yet
With eyes that keep them blind
But they grow and crystalize
Hiding from other creature in the sky

Escape from the smog
Take the risk
Find a flower that's safe
But this place can't always be the base

Don't be scared
Just leap, jump
Fall off the ledge
Better days are waiting ahead

You can fly
Peter Pan said you can
Soar to true beauty
That's why you have wings

--Emily Johnston

Regretting Roses

Uprooted in its lies
Its stem runs a mile long
Blooming among the other liars
That you find on Hollywood and Vine

The persona of delicate and soft
Virgin appeal in scent
Prickles down your fingertips
And the thrones stab you in

Red with flare
Delicate to fragile eyes
Bleeding crimson
With a detail for desire

--Emily Johnston

The Snake

Hiding beneath a pile of rocks
or cutting "S" curves in the sand
Seeking unsuspecting socks
where his fangs would like to land

He's a sly one-he's a killa
in the jungles of Manilla
Or the deserts dry and hot
scaly temper's what he's got

Rawest deal right from the start
the just result of being smart
Now because his plan went bust
he slithers wordless in the dust

When found in unsuspecting spot
the end result…he's usually shot!
Or unceremoniously chopped in half
with a shovel and a laugh

Even his name is thought of now
with degenerate lowest brow
When a person's on the take
he's only thought of as a snake!

--David Kettler

Cold Grass

I rake the falling amber leaves
With cascades more to come
But it really isn't pointless
To cold grass growing numb

The precious warmth of sunlight
Could mean life instead of death
To tender grass that's growing
In winter's chilling breath

Shoveling snow from the sidewalk
...another storm on the way
Certainly is not pointless
To the friends who are coming today

Cleaning things that will soil again
Washing what's been washed before
Pouring grain into an empty bin
Opening again the closing door

Teaching once more the lessons of life
Young ears have heard again & again
The same old stories that Grandpa told
Sometimes with a different spin

Adding more wood to the fires that burn
Knowing the dawn will bring cold
Sweetest slumber while clock dials turn
None are pointless...when the story's been told

It isn't pointless; it's not in vain
Labor that's done in the spirit of love
Bridges built or foundations lain
When prompted by the one above

--David Kettler

Crotalus scutulatus

Pardon its lethal dose, side-winding its way through California dystopia.
Forgive vicious flicking, glare sharp, piercing through thin skin,
Satisfying quick tantrums.
The real: do not tread on me.
It must resist, look for heat, sweltering, hissing,
Bit into every fiber of your identity.
Rattling against a temple, conveying power,
This pattern bursting on hazardous journey through golden state terra.

And I'm hissing now, I'm cold-blooded,
Minding my own, witness the dry storm of us.
Scales connecting brown skin,
Between ivory fang, poisonous to the veins,
Let me strike you. I will love you like you are non-threatening.

And the click-clack, is just my warning.
My tribal noise is just reminding you.
Leave me where I need be, and walk the other way,
You've done enough, your first error, was coming here.

Yellow eyes, fixed on radiating warmth, scent through my tongue,
I cannot let go, I remember what you taste of.

--Mateo Lara

Yerba Mansa

I will calm you. Te calmaré.
Perpetual, perennial at your hands.
I will stain this memory red.
I will fall crimson and swollen,
Autumn already sang my eternity.

Calming entangled worry, tangling through your bones,
Swarm and choke you out,
Engulf your Corazon, para siempre,
Breathe through any death.

I will close my eyes,
Dormant carvings pulse in my roots,
Spring will awaken me, and my love,
You'll bloom when a chill comes knocking,
Not any time before, supieras qué te esperaba.

This is my offering,
Colliding through a stream bed, seeping into your dampness,
That was your fingertips at my soil,
I will stain this memory red.
This is the marking you will bleed of for years.
It's beautiful, when you're not paying attention,
To this tranquility, forcing maturity, spreading us out.

--Mateo Lara

Wild Flower Lessons

Delicate petals, stems, stamen,
Intense colors,
Blue, purple, orange, magenta.
Fleeting beauty as days turn warm
Blossoms fade, turning to seed.

Look.
See.
Enjoy.
Drink in the beauty that is before you,
Made for your delight.

If you
        will only stop
                        your racing mind,

And be here now.

--Rose Lester

I AM

Surveying this vast expanse
I experience a sense of eternity.

The salty ocean spray mists my face.
I dig deep into the sand
to find the moisture below.
The beach is rich with life.
Sea gulls squawk overhead
Pelicans skydive for supper
while sand crabs burrow deep
Limpets and mussels cling desperately
to wave-worn rocks.
A shell tumbles towards the shore
pushed by the last big wave.

At water's edge, I yell in my biggest voice.
Fears, rage, sorrow,
hopes, longings and deepest desires
crashing out from a primal scream
Firmly and safely held by the powerful waves
and the thunderous sound of the surf.
The ocean holds them all.

Heaven and earth hear my prayer.
No more will I hide from life.
Transformation begins.
Dreaming turns into Doing.
Wishing becomes will-power.
Digging demands discovery.

I AM.

--Rose Lester

Sequoia (Sequoyah)

Standing watch for 3,000 years
Ring upon ring you have no peers
Should lighting flash a consuming fire

Your thick tannin filled bark
Holds back the flames spark
Fire sweeps leaving a mineral rich ground

Seeds by the thousands fall
Mother's tears nourish and call
Sprouts shoot up through earth

Drawing from Mother's deep well
You, a guardian spirit, towering dwell
So majestic you are granted a place

Extending year by year 50 feet higher
At your base, a city street could shelter
General Sherman your largest brother

Nature's skyscraper 26 stories high
Lace green dancing on wind's sigh
Deep is your breath, breathing earth

Rolling thunder, clapping call
Summer, Winter, Spring, Fall
Straight and true you rise

Writing your history in a language
Of your own, a story for ages
Each ring a layer revealing your truth

--Diane Lobre

Brother Crow

We hear your raucous call
Your twittering ruckus
Alarm, alarm you say

Yet you don't fly away
Instead you hop, hop
Cock your head
Hop, peck, hop, peck

It's said you are intelligent
You do listen intently
As your blackness reflects

Sunlight, highlighting
Your sleek back
Yet your large head
And squat body are comical

Up close you venture
We have legends about you
"Eat Crow" to be humbled

Some call you the "trickster"
Stealing bright shiny things
One of your brothers gave
My friend a feather meant for me

But it got lost before finding
It's way to me as a talisman
Another story to be told

Not rare or endangered
At least not anymore endangered
Than the rest of us
Your journey has been long

Traced back to Asia your cousins
Have spread to the Americas and beyond
How many secrets do you hold

You are not particular about

Home, you live in trees
In strip mall parking lots
At the gateway to Yosemite

Your very blackness signals
Alarm for those dressed in fear
As does your relative, Raven

Yet, underneath your feathers
Only bones, framing a bird
Blackness a symbol conjuring evil
Perception askew we flee

--Diane Lobre

Early Spring

Already in bloom again, the almonds
Standing in line
Wagging branches in petal-scattering wind and rain

Repeat what the almonds have been saying
For a century now, too quiet, too many,
too quick, too beautiful to be heard.

--Marit MacArthur

Kit Fox

It flickers across the field
Swiftly moving
As if its feet don't even touch the ground
Stops
And looks around
Head erect
Nose quivering
Tail swishing
Then it's off again
Like a dream sliding into consciousness
at the break of day
You try to grasp its meaning
but it slips away
Running on silent forefeet
the vision vanishes
Back into the realm of deep sleep
Will you ever glimpse it again?
Wait until dusk
When the kit fox emerges
And your mind reaches out once more
To grasp the elusive creature

--Carla Martin

Oleander Ladies

The hardy oleander bush
Flourishes along highways
Oblivious to the exhaust
Of passing automobiles
Vibrantly hued flowers
Bend on graceful stalks
Like the long-limbed ladies
That stroll along Union Avenue
They glance enticingly
At passing customers
Who will succumb to their charms?
Their leaves contain a poison
That projects their petals from feeling
The sharp stamen of intimacy
The hot anther of shame
The dust of the road
Clings to their stalks
These are tough flowers
As they satiate desperate desire
They bend and rise again
The oleander ladies

--Carla Martin

On the Outskirts at Spring

Blacked-eyed Susan – wake up – get off the ragged
carpet from where your husband knocked
the bloom off your face. Rise up in your shared
apartment, smelling of grit and gasoline.
This dirty town crushed by greed. Rise up!
Look through the window. Look past the empty

driveway to the vacant lot next to the out
of business day care where the black-eyed
Susans grow in the wrecked edges with one foot
outside the city limits. Go before the heat. Go
before the drought leaves birds thirsting, the trees
wilting, and all the flowers dying in the field.

Go.

--Jerry Mathes

Spring in the Garden

The perfume on the breeze attracts the killer
honey bee. The shock of its sting
and the gardener feels drunk among
the daisies and daffodils. The last
breathless curse at the edge where
black-eyed Susans stare blankly at the sun.
The high hum of short wings biting the air
fades as the bee sticky with pollen,
smelling of honey and springtime, falls.
Its body a smoke stained bullet casing.

--Jerry Mathes

Uprooted

My flora was a wildflower from
Guatemala. She taught me her
language of bare roots
and ginger drinks. Her scent
lofted through open doors and
careless screens where she'd grin
and grind her teeth.

My flora
opened at night to the twilights
of warm winters and kitchen
sinks. Like the purple needle grass
she swayed to midnight melody. Roots
Seized discovery – migrating her
on warm winds, with thrill
she left me in the California desert -
a sunken sea.

--Chyna Parker

poodle ponderings, perspective per pepper

pressing my paws against those pages that physically pain you,
whimpering under my breath to remind you,
that i too am helpless.
But my starvation is a direct result of your oppression,
and i need you to quit that human suffering studies,
utilize those opposable thumbs to tip that bag into my bowl.
i will personally buy mr biswas that damned house,
if you would please leash me and allow me the luxury of pissing on those
          greens
in the field where those black and white cats startle you as the sun sets.

--Shelby Pinkham

neglected notion native to the nursery

extending my evergreen blades beyond this base,
that bestows ethereal experiences upon brains.
breathing without beat,
is my victory and my defeat.
for i am without a voice to whisper,
that i too am helpless.
But my thirst is in direct consequence of your depression,
and i need you to quit that human suffering studies,
utilize your spinal cord to bend to the earth extending nourishment.
i will personally feed rukmani's entire family,
if you would please prevent that four-legged beast from pissing on me,
in the field where those black and white cats startle you as the sun sets.

--Shelby Pinkham

Ochotona

Politically unknown hands and feet roam through light
Integrity fades in the wake of the kingdom
Keywords unspoken spill through open cracks of dust
Abides the unjust routine of the comfortable

--Nashwa Rafiq

Helianthus

Darkness concealed underneath a coat of happiness
Simply round walls closing in
Hidden sharp thorns embrace the thunder
Marked with the enemy's touch
Sky-high shadow stands near behind a loud yellow
A trail of casualties know by heart
Voices buried beneath rubble

--Nashwa Rafiq

Orgasms

I blessed you with my orgasms
Not merely out of satisfaction,
But because it was a
Pleasant attraction,
It was my gift to provide
Not lend,
Contribution as a whole,
Isn't that what the sun offers,
Isn't that how the soil prospers,
Opening,
Giving,
Vastly cultivated,
Until it is seemingly voided.
For instance,
The Mariposa Lily,
A Sierra Nevada native,
Whose delicate appearance cannot be fooled,
It survives wildfires,
It grows from an underground bulb,
Maturing,
Blooming,
Only within time,
Its own time,
Timing so perfect
It outlasts where others debilitated
And could not grow.
And when it slows,
It is uniquely thriving in hope.
And please
Do not mistake void for emptiness,
A surface is faint certainty
And
It was overflowing underneath,
Denying the burn to destroy,
Instead,
It would anoint,
But only after the fire was contained,
Only after the destruction was restrained,
Only after the claim of
A prosperous seed.
The unseen

Evocative--
I bet you can still feel it.
The seconds urging
And
Brilliantly aching
When a cocoon has bursts,
When wings have radiated power,
And
I instinctively nurtured
Your thirst,
Furiously painting --
The way my earthly healing
Exudes-
What a miracle it is
To be born
After a burn,
beneath the dirt....
Yo naci de un fuego.
Precisely
How
An abundance of orgasms
become
A treasured birth.

--Diana Ramirez

Homeless

I saw you--kit fox.
Roaming.
Union Avenue and Brundage Lane.
This morning--kit fox.
Roaming.
East Truxtun Avenue.
Last night--kit fox.
Roaming.
Corners off the freeway.
But you never stay
Because you roam.
Wander
From streetlight to streetlight,
No charge spared,
Asphalt broken,
And the next corner
Might be the token
To a meal,
A cast-iron scorn,
Or a makeshift bed.
I'm not sure what you said,
But
I see you,
Wide-eyed,
Quick stride,
Hoping to find
An answer--perhaps.
I wish I had the answer.
I can barely spare a quarter.
I'm sorry--kit fox.
I am witness to your
Diminished habitat.
You alone
Create your home
As you roam--
Kit fox.
I don't blame you.
For treading
For fleeing,
And never remaining,
You're visibly weary,

The miles keep adding up,
The temperatures are dropping,
And I can't imagine how much you shiver.
I can't imagine how much you pray.
I can't imagine being castaway.

And the rest of us--kit fox.
We remain.
Remain closed.
Remain rejecting.
Remain snug.
Oh, what lovely
Creatures we are,
Creatures of habit.
Arm's length to change.

I don't blame you--kit fox.
For running away.

--Diana Ramirez

Sun's Flower

Stand tall and proud with slender arms outstretched
and graceful neck bend and tilt your face
your golden face
up to the sun for love's true kiss
and fierce your heart
a warrior's one
let never wilt but instead stand firm

Be gentle too and listen
to the words of your dear friends
that Butterfly sends
from one to another as he flits
his wings across your face

Pipe these messages to the ground
to the souls that lie below
and take my message to the grave
of my dearest one beneath

--Bailey Russell

A Wild Chase

Coyote stood upon the hill
the short hill really more a mound
and sniffed the air
to search and find
Roadrunner as he darted by

A whiff he caught upon the breeze
and darted out on sandy seas
of dirt dry from lack of rain
his footprints standing out
on hard-packed ground.

Roadrunner zoomed past
Coyote's gaping jaws
with speed so fast dust
billowed in the air
a jet trail of desert sand

He dashed further still
lest he be caught
followed by the sound
of Coyote's wild howls.

Squirrel ran in the street
scaring the life out of Driver
dodging tires at the last second
standing on the roadside
looking back at her to gloat

But when Coyote howled
Squirrel skittered up the tree
and there he sought shelter from
the teeth that threatened him
Squirrel called it running for his life
Driver called it karma for his deeds.

--Bailey Russell

Beauty and the Beast

Oh, the undeniable beauty surrounds us here in Kern County.
Burning orange poppies and romantic blue-purple lupine,
Lemony yellow buttercups and brilliant white popcorn flowers,
Vivid green miners lettuce and golden hills of dry grasses.
Yet hidden from our view lurks the ugliest native beast...
This beast lies in wait for its unsuspecting victims, human and animal,
It is in many of us, never even noticed,
Oh, but just wait...
When you least suspect it...
WHAM!!
It grabs you in the lungs and viscously spreads systemically in some,
Attacking the brain, bones, heart and other organs.
So soak in the vast beauty of Kern County, but
Beware of the BEAST...
VALLEY FEVER.

--Caroline Russell

Diversity

Scampering up and down evergreens,
Tails flicking, cheeks filling.
Pine cones dropping, now deformed,
Cal State University Bakersfield squirrels traverse the campus.
Elsewhere skirt shy large-eared kit foxes,
Eyes wide seeing all,
Commonly hiding in earthen dens,
Coexisting with professors, coeds, and staff.
Seeking and snagging worms and insects near Middle Earth,
Robin Red Breasts catch their fill.
Oh the beauty of nature at our feet,
Before our eyes and above our heads,
All found in the heart of town.
Truly, CSUB is home to a diverse community,
Yet we can still do more to
Respect and protect all of God's creatures.
Sharing this habitat with large sharp eared, bright eyed tiny kit foxes.
Robin Red Breasts seek and snag earth worms and a variety of insects.

--Caroline Russell

One Stalk for All the State

Standing Proud and strong
In the field beneath the sun
On the mountainside
In the day and in the night
Swaying gently with the breeze
A vibrant orange
Like the fire, like the dawn,
Deep green too as the verdant grass
Reaching for the sky, never trembling
Signaling the power and the grace
Of the entire state and all its glory
And the majesty of a mother so enduring
Even in the driest years,
Yes, even in the drought
Still quietly standing, never stirring
Though lessened mass not at all diminished
In the eye of the beholder
A symbol of so much
Yet so little of frame, of stature
This is the California Poppy.

--Sidney Russell

The Day of Fauna

It was three a.m. when I awoke to a shrill chirping sound.
The cricket in his small abode ran round and round.
His legs rubbed together, and sound ushered forth.
I moaned; I groaned. It was too early to get up!

At four o'clock the cat came in.
She meowed in my ear, her tail swishing back and forth,
Softly purring; I didn't want to hear.
I stumbled from my bed and got the food.
The cats pointed ears were twitching.
She hissed; I groaned. It was too early for all of this!

A squeaking sound, a long slim tail,
Teeth gleaming in the dark,
The source of Kitty's disposition slithered into view:
A rat of course.
It ran; I groaned. It was too early for a chase!

By the time the rat was gone, it was half-past six o'clock.
Tweeting, chirping in the trees signaled the birds were rising.
Graceful wings and gentle beaks peaked out among the branches.
They sang; I groaned. It was time to get up.

After breakfast and a hasty dash, I made it just in time to class
When out the window the professor glanced.
"Oh my! What's that?" she asked.
The class turned and I as well to see.
It was nothing more than the old kit fox running beneath the trees:
Here and there a fluffy tail, scrawny body, foxlike head.
The class laughed; I groaned. Why was I still up?

Before my head could rest upon the inviting desk,
A shout rang out, "Look, there!" and I obliged.
A marathon of roadrunners darted past.
They were tall and strong though seeming small.
Their heads held high and feathers ruffled were a sight of pride.
I didn't moan; I didn't groan. It was worth it to be up!

--Sidney Russell

Sequence In Which The Roots Could Be
Praying For Us

1. Burned Chaparral

The deep roots could be praying
Inaudibly, taking time
From their own slow recovery
To make intercession for ours.

2. Uprooted

The wreckage of this almond grove,
Dead leaves the color of dried blood,
Shouldn't trouble anyone—unless
Every loss reminds you of all losses.

3. Mesquite

The sparse shade beneath it tattered
Like rotten cloth, it has nothing to offer.
Dry branches twist in on themselves,
Choosing half-death as a way of life.

4. Underground

Among things that feed on light,
Communion: faith in rain,
Fear of drought, of fire and pale nodes
For which there is no known cure.

5. Semiotic

In the rain, burnt umber nut trees
Finally come to the dark end
Of the brown scale. That means
We'll see leaf buds in less than a month.

6. Faith

From here to the barren hills,
Nothing but sand grass and thistles—
Except for one spindly mesquite
With roots six inches deeper than doubt.

--Don Thompson

Sequence In Which Life Goes On
Beneath Our Notice

1. Ontogeny Recaps Phylogeny

No one unable to quiet his or her mind
Ever disrespects insects, those restless
Distant cousins of thought
Skittering among blades of grass.

2. Carapace

Even our unassuming local beetles
Astound listless senses
When we turn a rock over and see
Electric jade shimmering on obsidian.

3. Spared

Under such an inconclusive moon,
Not ever the owl can act,
But flies back and forth above the field.
The mice will go home tonight.

4. Residual

Tawny grass still grows tall here
That hid cougars a hundred years ago.
Nothing in it now but an insect hum
And fear too deep inside us to deny.

5. Spoils

Down in the kingdom of blue-green beetles,
No king. His carapace
Glistens like a priceless Fabergé egg
On Display in the museum of the ants.

6. Spider

Light exists at this moment
Only to glisten on the filament
By which a spider descends
To take hold of the earth.

--Don Thompson

The Startling Wild Grasses of Amsterdam

To Frances Young,
wounded healer

I've never been to Amsterdam.
But fall's perhaps penultimate
fly on my ear, the wild potted
grasses on the afternoon patio,
with their moment-by-moment
reinvention of light, illumined
purples with greens as their
boundaries and seams, speak
not only of Anne Frank in her
attic but of each indigenous
flower in Amsterdam braving
snow not only to resurrect but
    to remember.

--Tim Vivian

Descant

Do you see that one, afternoon, bird
now glancing from branch to scalded
branch, each movement mourning loss
and yet, still, celebrating birth? Two
motions that neither you nor I will
ever understand. Do you see that bird
of paradise, flowering into senescence?

It, in and of itself, is miracle. No, don't
go on pilgrimage to far-off Galilee, or
far within what doctors can't discern.
Look at each vertiginous yet solid hue,
admire each deep-veined advance and
withdrawal. When all our armies throw
down their arms, then, and only then,
will this our bird sing us to its descant.

--Tim Vivian

California Cockroach

brown as backyard bark,
blond as golden wheat,
black as dark drains,
you scurry in the garage,
hide through the cracks,
stare me straight in the eye,
under a pesticide spell,
and await my hoover wind tunnel.

out of the ships of europe's sails you came,
my ancestors should have squashed you.
inside the spice bags of india's shores,
my brothers should have smothered you.
out of the copper mines of timbuktu,
my mothers should have destroyed you.

but still you ride on the backs of rats,
you travel far and abroad,
from the west to the orient
drinking spilled drinks on a perpetual holiday.

disease ridden,
winged and armored,
cockamaney pest --

get off my apple peel.

--Jana Lee Wong

Yucca Plant

your name is so opposite
of your white, flowering beauty,
strong survivor of the california drought,
soapy cleanser of the body,
sustenance of man, tasty root,
sharp thread, needle included.
.

you undoubtedly stabbed a
conquistador or two, oh spanish dagger,
happily slowing their pace toward
enslavement of the natives.

you are nature's star on top
the ravaged mountain,
the hope which springs,
a guiding attendant in the desert.

your blossoms stand tall to the wind,
tuliped damsels over guards of spikes,
witch of wondrous remedies,
Antioxidant, antifungal,
one with the earth,
sprouted hair washed in water,
a thousand times curled,
one hundred yuccas thriving
over a blistering landscape.

the conquistadors are
absorbed into the fabric
of multicultural complexities,
but you, yucca, are timeless,
unchanging under a lightning sky.

--Jana Lee Wong

Indeterminate Unity

Datura wrigjtii fondles roadside sandy washes,
leaves pumping atropine and scopolamine,
the night's engorged white-lipped trumpets.

The Toloache's north-root

suppresses eye saccades,
induces a functional blindness,
enables visual and auditory hallucinations.

Do you see it?

Thus would the Yokut and Mohave mine flight

and be else.

The Western Jimsonweed's primary pollinator
sphinx moth, *Maduca rustica*
unfurls a proboscis thrice its body length
tongues the nectar nestled in those whorled folds.

In Georgia O'Keefe's . . .

. . . *Jimson Weed, 1932*, the mind's five slender teeth,
the canvas cultivated on stamen and pistil
as if the sex were an herbaceous eye.

. . . *Jimson Weed, 1936*, clock-step,
the corollae grasp and enjoin the pupil
to fuse and seed.

If I could paint the flower exactly as I see it
no one would see what I see
because I would paint it small
like the flower is small.

Do you see it?

The moon blooms.
We gasp ourselves awake.

--Matthew Woodman

(An earlier version of this poem appeared in the journal *El Portal* 72.1. 2015)

Friend of the Birds
        (after Rufino Tamayo's *Amigo de los pájaros*, 1944)

use the extension ladder
to reach the skylight where

hummingbirds would exhaust
themselves collapsing grasp

them loosely a thumb of fire
descend aluminum one foot

before a time comes choose
the weather drought deluge

the landscape before you
and whether to care

for what flies for what
falls if you're not there

--Matthew Woodman

About the Authors

A young author, **Sera Bethany** is highly academic-oriented and enjoys learning for the sake of wisdom. A large amount of her time is spent traveling and collecting folklore past and present which often inspires her works in one way or another. Her interests, however, extend far beyond the humanities alone and into nearly every aspect of every subject from ancient and modern language to history, music, math, physics, and far beyond. After all, her motto in life was, is, and shall remain τῷ σοφῷ ξένον οὐδέν.

Sherean Bledsoe is the Administrative Support Coordinator for the Department of Mathematics at California State University, Bakersfield, and working towards her undergraduate degree in Public Administration.

Greg C. Bolanos is a CSUB alumni with a bachelor's degree in Theatre; he's written and produced multiple short films with the help of the CSUB Film Club and has had two plays produced locally. He plans to continue his career as a writer until the overwhelming pressure to write drives him into an early grave.

Portia Choi devotes her time promoting poetry by hosting the monthly First Friday Open Mic and publicizing events during National Poetry Month in April. She administers www.kernpoetry.com with stories and pictures of poets and poetry events. She published a chapbook of her poems *Sungsook, Korean War Poems*. She is published in in *Orpheus*, *The Asian Pacific American Journal*, *KoreAm Journal*, *A Sharp Piece of Awesome*, *Primary Point*, *Writers of Kern Anthology*, *Emeritus Voices*, *Levan Humanities Review*, and *Invisible Memoirs*. Choi previously worked in Public Health. She can be reached at portia@kernpoetry.com

Priti Devaprakash is a 21-year-old transfer English major who studied Biology in her previous college life, still loves music, and still is trying to find a career that brings together both science and art. She is also an avid lover of animals (esp. dogs), books, philosophy, film and exploring the beauty and the tragedy of the human condition.

When he isn't fishing obscure stretches of the Kern River, **Jeff Eagan** is the Writing Center/Tutoring Coordinator and teaches English at CSUB. He loves comics, David Bowie, and eating food that will probably kill him.

Zeltzin Estrada-Rodriguez is a learner, a lover, a woman who embraces life and strives to have an positive impact on the environment around her. Perhaps most importantly, perhaps least, she is a writer. Through the stories she shares she hopes to encourage people everywhere to open their minds and hearts to new lifestyles, ideas, and forms of expression.

This is **Shelley Evans'** third year at CSUB's April poetry reading, and she enjoys the challenge of writing with a theme in mind. Many of her poems are inspired by the beach and are often written with her feet in the Pismo sand. She can also be found in Dagnys at open mic night on First Fridays and at monthly Writers of Kern meetings. You may hear her rhyming along in life, as she tells you "Write On!"

Andrea Franco is a third year English major undecided of what she would like to pursue as a career after college. Despite this uncertainty, she does know one thing- she expects to work in a field that allows freedom of expression.

Tea connoisseur and sushi-serving extraordinaire **Karissa Garcia** thoroughly enjoys all things artistic. A hopeless romantic at heart, Karissa spends her days eagerly searching for the next adventure. She sing-songs her way through life, and is a firm believer that beauty can be found in unexpected places. Karissa thrives when drawing, singing, running, yoga-ing, eating, movie-watching, trying new things and creating sick playlists on Spotify. She waits for the song to end before leaving the car, and will call you when the moon looks especially beautiful.

Jack Hernandez writes in cafes and coffee shops. His caffeine inspired poems have appeared in journals like *A Sharp Piece of Awesome* and the *Anglican Theological Review*. He is currently the Director of the Norman Levan Center of the Humanities at Bakersfield College.

Anke Hodenpijl is a writer, poet, paddler of global waters, and outdoor enthusiast. She is a retired business owner, teacher and behavioral analyst. She is especially proud of reading her poetry at the 2018 Bakersfield Women's March. Her work appears in various journals, ezines and newspapers. Currently she volunteers with the Bakersfield Threshold Singers, the Bakersfield Art and Spirituality Center, and works with survivors of human trafficking, using poetry as a means to heal and find peace. She may be reached at ahodenpijl@gmail.com.

Chad Johnson is frequently unemployed and yet never without work to do. Whether you love or hate his work, he's happy you care enough to form an opinion.

Once a literary snob, **Emily Johnston** has escaped the realm of amateur hour to rise above the mediocracy as a pretentious poet.

When not lifting heavy batteries for his day job, **David Kettler** enjoys writing poetry, authoring books, or building metal sculpture pieces. *One Smart Antelope*, *My Reasons in Rhyme* and *Heavy Metaling* are three of his books that are available on Amazon. He has been writing poetry since he was very young and still does when inspiration strikes.

Mateo Lara enjoys cheap wine and bad horror movies when he isn't writing poetry or being a bad person while trying to be a good person. He believes life, in general, is work, so we're constantly busy one way or another for someone or something. His poems have appeared in *The New Engagement* and *Orpheus,* and he has published two poetry books--*Keta-Miha and Other Poems* and *La Futura Tuga*--and one chapbook--*X, Marks the Spot*--all available on Amazon.

Rose Lester is a Marriage Family Therapist in private practice. When not seeing clients, she loves all things creative and expresses herself in many different artistic mediums. Her poems have been published in several anthologies and online websites. She volunteers for the Art for Healing program at Mercy Hospital. She can be reached at rosemft@att.net

Diane Lobre retired from the Hawai`i Public Health Institute (HIPHI), where she assisted with its mission of providing education and advocacy leadership on key public health issues such as tobacco control. She lived and worked in Hawai`i for 27 years. Reading and writing are her favorite pastimes. She has written poetry from a young age along with a few short stories, is a graduate of North High School and Bakersfield Community College (BC), and worked for BC for 14 years prior to moving to Hawai`i. She enjoys learning and frequents the Art & Spirituality Center for painting, writing and meditation classes.

Carla Martin is a substitute teacher by day and a poet and children's story writer by night. She is a regular performer at Dagney's Open Mic Poetry Readings on First Fridays in Downtown Bakersfield. Carla is a member of Writers of Kern and Society of Children's Book Writers and Illustrators. You can read more of her poetry and prose at www.carlajoypoetry.com.

Marit MacArthur is Professor of English at California State University, Bakersfield. She holds a B.A. in English and creative writing at Northwestern University, a Ph.D. in English from UC Davis, and a MFA from Warren Wilson College. Her poems and translations from the Polish have appeared in *Southwest Review*, *Leveler*, *Front Porch*, *Jacket2*, *American Poetry Review*, *Watershed Review*, *World Literature Today*, *Verse*, *ZYZZYVA*, *Peregrine*, the *Levan Humanities Review*, and *Airplane Reading*.

Chyna Parker is a master's student who admires the art of writing; she hopes to use her passion for poetry in her career as a Licensed Marriage and Family Therapist. Chyna has been published by *Hinchas de Poesia*, *Orpheus*, and *One Book, One Bakersfield, One Kern*.

Shelby Pinkham is an English major, but that's really just a hobby. She is making a half-assed living as a beer snob. She has had one previous poem published, but don't bother looking for it. In her free time she is pretending to write a book.

When **Nashwa Rafiq** isn't hard at work writing meaningful poems or expressing herself through art, She works as a Payment Services student assistant. A junior at CSUB, she is a Liberal Studies and Sociology major with a minor in Art.

Being a mother is her motivation, community is her drive, and life is her inspiration. **Diana Ramirez** works for local non-profit CASA of Kern County and is a Bakersfield College student. She is also a Board member for the Arts Council of Kern and for Bakersfield Parent Nursery. Her love of poetry, spoken word, and art inspired her to begin Words Come to Life in 2016--a poetry-inspired art event. Catch her on the road driving part-time for Uber, exploring BookHounds with her two boys, or admiring the clouds in the sky. Daydreaming has always been her strong suit.

Bailey Russell aspires to become an author and pediatrician. She hopes to open a private practice with her twin sister, which will later be expanded into a quality care clinic for people in the community who struggle financially and could not otherwise afford quality medical care. Her hobbies include reading, writing, and singing, and she loves to meet new people. In addition to reading and writing, she can often be found studying, working at the Writing Resource Center, or spending time with her family. She intends to obtain a Ph.D. in English – either medieval literature or philology – prior to attending medical school for her M.D., and loves reading mythology and folklore.

Caroline Russell, a Type 1 Diabetic since 1974, has lived in Kern County almost all her life. In her youth, she attended San Diego State University, studying Psychology, Journalism, and Photography as well as taking on the role of President of the Public Relations Student Society of America. She went on to earn her Teaching Credential at Chapman College in 1987 before leading a fulfilling career as an elementary school teacher and later the leader of a Children's Liturgy Program at St. John the Evangelist Parish in Wasco, CA. Still, she says she didn't know what life and true happiness were until she had her first child at the age of 29½. Her kids are now the focus of her life, and daughters Bailey and Sidney are her inspiration and joy. She loves being around people and being in nature, though her outings have been limited lately due to contracting and battling Valley Fever.

Sidney Russell is an aspiring pediatrician and author. In the future, she hopes to open a practice with her twin sister and eventually expand it into a quality care facility for people who cannot otherwise afford medical care. She enjoys reading, writing, and meeting new people. When not reading or writing, she is typically studying, working at the Writing Resource Center on campus, or spending time with her family. Before going on to pursue her M.D., she will work toward a Ph.D. in English – medieval literature or philology, and she is always on the prowl for a good mythology book.

Don Thompson has been writing about the San Joaquin Valley for over fifty years, including a dozen or so books and chapbooks. His most recent release is *From Here On: Four Sunday Drives*. For more info and links to publishers, visit his website at www.don-e-thompson.com.

Tim Vivian has published numerous books, article, and book reviews in his academic field of study, early Christian monasticism. He has lately turned more attention to literary efforts, publishing articles on the poetry of Denise Levertov and Rowan Williams and on the novels of Marilynne Robinson. You may reach him at tvivian@csub.edu.

Jana Lee Wong has poems appearing in *The Levan Humanities Review* and *The California Quarterly of Poetry* including "Letting Go," about the love for her daughter, "Soul Mate," a tribute to her husband, and "Time on Monk's Hill," about seeking truth and inspiration. By day, she teaches seventh and eighth graders at Standard Middle School, and by night, she teaches English at Bakersfield College. Her hobbies include traveling, swimming, hiking, cycling, and writing science fiction and poetry. She can be reached at jana.wong@bakersfieldcollege.edu.

When he is not practicing crow calls, **Matthew Woodman** teaches writing at CSUB and is the founding editor of the journal *Rabid Oak*. More of his words can be found at www.matthewwoodman.com.

Community Partners

Without like-minded accomplices, an artist would be little more than a voice in the wilderness, writing, creating, and reciting for an audience of stone and wind. Thankfully, we have those accomplices that keep us energized and connected.

Thank you to our literary community partners, who are making Bakersfield and Kern County more vibrant, more imaginative, more inclusive, more beautiful.

Writers of Kern (WOK) is a branch of the California Writers Club (CWC). One of the nation's oldest professional clubs for writers, CWC was founded by Jack London and fellow writers in 1909 for the purpose of helping aspiring authors socialize with published authors.

The Writers of Kern is a non-profit organization bringing together professional writers and novice writers in a creative and supportive atmosphere. Published writers share their knowledge and skills through critique groups, at general meetings and during conferences and workshops, and non-published writers gain experience, encouragement, and guidance to help them become published writers. Meetings and critique groups are positive, uplifting events meant to inspire and motivate all writers to dedicate time to the fulfilling craft of writing.

For more information, visit writersofkern.com

FIRST FRIDAY Open Mic is held every First Friday at 6:00 p.m. at Dagny's Coffee in Downtown Bakersfield.

The sign-in for the free and public Open Mic is at Dagny's on the night of the event. On most evenings, there is a featured poet or a musician.

For more information, contact Portia at portia@kernpoetry.com

Sponsored by Dagny's Coffee and Kern Poetry

Recent Publications by Our Contributors

Every Library needs to grow, to breathe, to expand. Add to your
library with these recent publications by some of our authors.

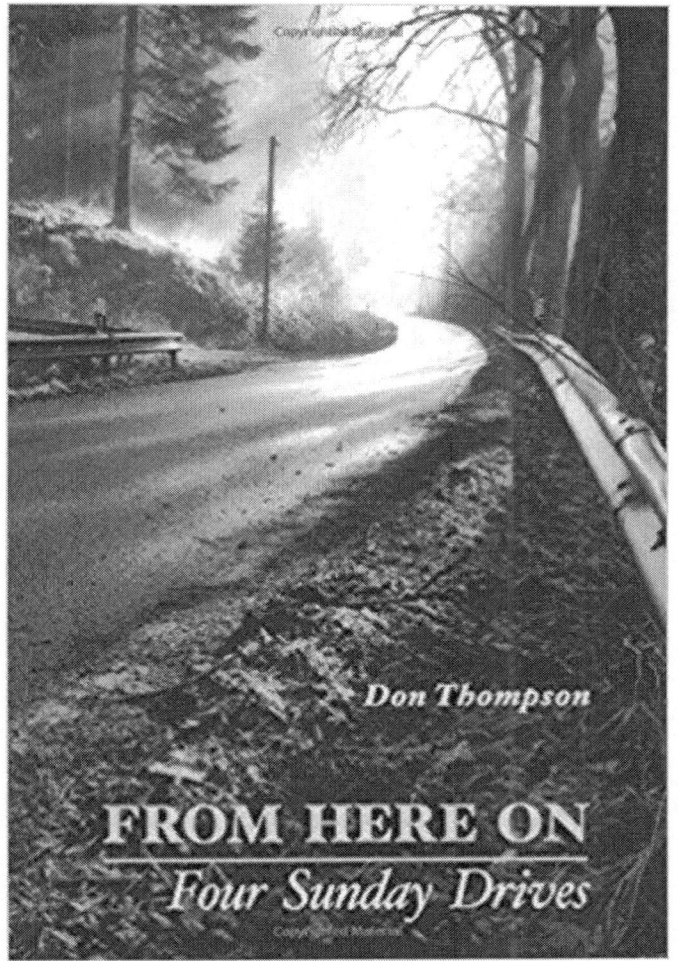

FROM HERE ON
Four Sunday Drives

Kern County Poet Laureate Don Thompson is a native of the southern San Joaquin Valley where he has lived most of his life, writing about its unique environment. In *From Here On: Four Sunday Drives*, he revives an old tradition, documenting road trips to nearby farmland, the foothills, and to the Sierras. Thompson reflects on the passing of time and the deterioration and abuse of the land. Even in the outlying areas reached only on back roads, there is evidence of vandalism and violence. And yet the landscape he loves somehow endures.

"If there was an official poet laureate of the West, Don Thompson would be my choice. For four decades he has reminded us what it means to be alive out here, coping with a world we do not fully understand. In *Local Color*, he employs an original format to present, as usual, wonderful word-pictures. Also as usual, "place" is a character in his work, but not just any place: the south San Joaquin with all its peculiarities and wonders. No writer has seen more there or told more telling tales as a result. This is narrative poetry that really narrates!"

—Gerald Haslam, author of *Straight White Male* and *Leon Patterson: a California Story*

In this North American Award winning memoir, Jerry D. Mathes II takes readers into the heart of wildfires from the forests of Idaho to the deserts of the Mexican border—and directly into the lives of the men and women who face the terror, beauty, and hardship of life on the fire line. His story testifies to their extraordinary camaraderie, forged by thunderstorms that scatter lightning and hail, high summer heat and shivering nights in which bears prowl through wilderness camps, and quiet days of reflection, waiting for what may come next.

With a poet's lyricism, Mathes tells of the life and death of friends, of negotiating the bureaucracy of the federal fire service, and of the rivalry of competing agencies. He wistfully describes the weighty absence of his daughters as they grow up and the desperate feeling of failure even as he appears to be succeeding. Readers live alongside Mathes as he grows from a stunned rookie trembling under arcing flames into a seasoned member of the training cadre. His life comes full circle when he brings his hard-won field experience back to the classroom, giving his students the tools to work and survive in the chaotic world of wilderness wildfires.

In *Shipwrecks and Other Stories*, we read of men and women struggling in love and longing, adultery and addiction, between staying in a place and moving on, while trying to rediscover who they are. Characters in these tales haunt the fringes of their own lives shipwrecked in society as they seek identity, hoping to rescue themselves.

"Shipwrecks is chock-full of rough lives and hard times, yet these stories are laced with hope and threaded through with moments of grace. With his intimate knowledge of the natural world, from the desert to the sea, Mathes creates vivid settings, sometimes malevolent, sometimes benign, but always a presence to be reckoned with. Like Stephen Crane and Raymond Carver before him, Mathes shines the harsh light of realism on the daily conflicts, large and small, that define his characters' fears and desires and, often, determine their very survival."

−Kim Barnes, author of *In the Kingdom of Men* and *In the Wilderness*

With friendship and love, comes change and growth. This chapbook swarms with the ideas of passion, friendship, love, pain, change, and how to devote yourself to someone in the midst of life and its never-ending source of woe. *X, Marks the Spot* aims to pay homage to the beauty of friendship, the pain of love, and the hope for connection even after something has broken.

Memories are like bone. With this collection of poetry, Lara attempts to traverse the landscape of pain, heartbreak, friendship, piece it together into one body of remembrance. The skeleton of history, heritage, and secrets that would rather be forgotten.

Start drafting and revising for 2019's edition . . .

WRITING SOUND

Made in the USA
San Bernardino, CA
07 March 2018